Buddy BOOKS
Prehistoric Animals

Short-faced Bear

ABDO
Publishing Company

A Buddy Book
by
Michael P. Goecke

VISIT US AT
www.abdopub.com

Published by Buddy Books, an imprint of ABDO Publishing Company, 4940 Viking Drive, Edina, Minnesota 55435. Copyright © 2004 by Abdo Consulting Group, Inc. International copyrights reserved in all countries. No part of this book may be reproduced in any form without written permission from the publisher.

Printed in the United States.

Edited by: Christy DeVillier
Contributing Editor: Matt Ray
Graphic Design: Deborah Coldiron
Image Research: Deborah Coldiron
Illustrations: Deborah Coldiron, Denise Esner
Photographs: Corbis, Corel, Minden Pictures, Photodisc

Library of Congress Cataloging-in-Publication Data

Goecke, Michael P., 1968-
    Short-faced bear / Michael P. Goecke.
      p. cm. — (Prehistoric animals. Set II)
    Summary: Introduces the physical characteristics, habitat, and behavior of the prehistoric relative of modern-day bears.
    Includes bibliographical references and index.
    ISBN 1-57765-976-7
    1. Giant short-faced bear—Juvenile literature. [1. Giant short-faced bear. 2. Mammals, Fossil. 3. Prehistoric animals. 4. Paleontology.] I. Title.

QE882.C15 G646 2003
569'.78—dc21

                        2002032278

Table of Contents

Prehistoric Animals

Scientists say that Earth is more than four billion years old. Long before people, many kinds of animals lived here. Animals that lived more than 5,500 years ago are prehistoric. Dinosaurs, woolly mammoths, and saber-toothed cats were all prehistoric animals.

Dinosaurs were around millions of years ago.

Prehistoric Animals

The Short-faced Bear

Short-faced bears were prehistoric animals. They were deadly predators. Short-faced bears may have been the largest bears that ever lived. Some people call them bulldog bears.

Scientists have names for important time periods in Earth's history. The short-faced bear lived during a time period called the Pleistocene. The Pleistocene began about two million years ago.

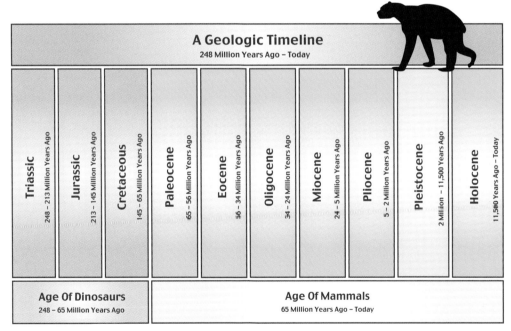

A Geologic Timeline
248 Million Years Ago – Today

Triassic 248 – 213 Million Years Ago	**Jurassic** 213 – 145 Million Years Ago	**Cretaceous** 145 – 65 Million Years Ago	**Paleocene** 65 – 56 Million Years Ago	**Eocene** 56 – 34 Million Years Ago	**Oligocene** 34 – 24 Million Years Ago	**Miocene** 24 – 5 Million Years Ago	**Pliocene** 5 – 2 Million Years Ago	**Pleistocene** 2 Million – 11,500 Years Ago	**Holocene** 11,500 Years Ago – Today

Age Of Dinosaurs
248 – 65 Million Years Ago

Age Of Mammals
65 Million Years Ago – Today

Short-faced bears lived between 800,000 and 10,000 years ago.

7

What It Looked Like

Short-faced bears did not have a tall forehead. This is why scientists call them "short-faced."

Short-faced bears were taller than today's brown bears. They had longer legs. Short-faced bears were slimmer than brown bears, too.

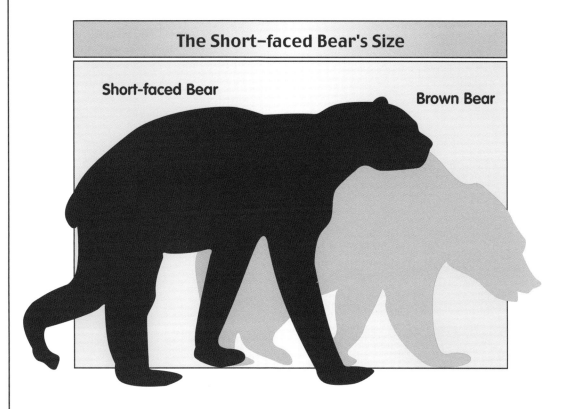

The Short–faced Bear's Size

Short-faced Bear

Brown Bear

    Short-faced bears could grow to become more than five feet (two m) tall. An adult standing on its back legs was about 11 feet (3 m) tall. Short-faced bears weighed about 1,500 pounds (680 kg). The females were smaller than the males.

The short-faced bear was a large prehistoric predator.

Animals with long legs and short faces are commonly fast. This is true for today's African lions. So scientists believe short-faced bears were fast runners, too.

African lions are fast enough to catch zebras.

Today's brown bears are pigeon-toed. They walk and run with their toes pointing inward. Brown bears can run as fast as 30 miles (48 km) per hour.

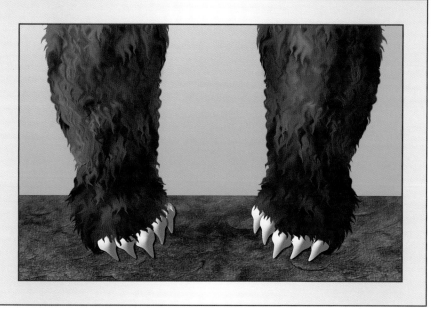

Pigeon-toed

Brown bears walk with their toes pointing inward.

Short-faced bears were not pigeon-toed. They walked and ran with their toes pointing forward. This may have allowed them to run faster than brown bears.

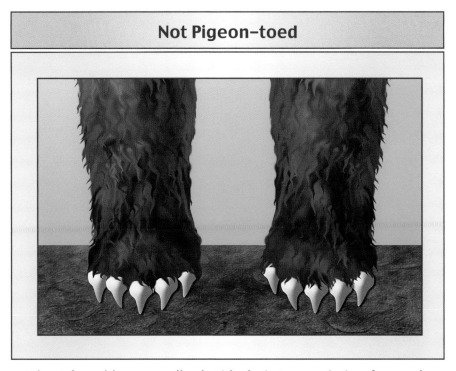

Not Pigeon–toed

Short-faced bears walked with their toes pointing forward.

13

Fun Facts

Spectacled Bears

Today's spectacled bears are related to short-faced bears. Spectacled bears are named after the circles around their eyes. These bears live in South America. They eat plants, insects, and small animals. Unlike short-faced bears, they spend most of their time in trees.

This spectacled bear is related to the short-faced bear.

Strong Predator

Short-faced bears were powerful predators. They probably hunted bison, caribou, deer, and horses. Short-faced bears may have eaten plants, too.

Scientists believe short-faced bears had a keen sense of smell. They may have had good eyesight, too. These senses would help short-faced bears find prey.

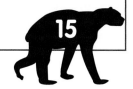

15

Scientists believe the short-faced bear had a strong bite. Its head was like a lion's head in some ways. Lions have muscles that help them bite down hard. Short-faced bears may have had strong muscles for biting, too.

Lions have a strong bite.

Short-faced Bear's World

Short-faced bears lived during the Ice Age. During that time, the world cooled. Giant sheets of ice covered many lands.

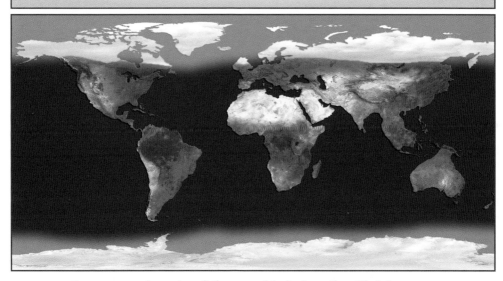

The Pleistocene World

Ice covered parts of the world during the Pleistocene.

17

Short-faced bears lived in North America's woodlands and grasslands. Some lived as far north as Alaska and Canada. Others lived as far south as Mexico. Many lived throughout what is now the United States.

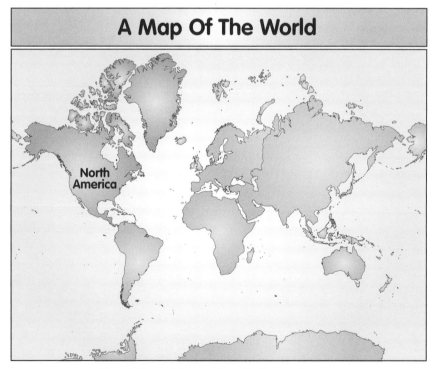

A Map Of The World

North America

Short-faced bear fossils have been found throughout North America.

Brown bears and black bears lived in North America during the Pleistocene, too. They probably ate the same things as short-faced bears. Some scientists believe there was not enough food for all the bears. Maybe this is why short-faced bears died out about 10,000 years ago.

Brown bears (left) and black bears (right) are still around today.

People have found millions of fossils at the Rancho La Brea Tar Pits. Some of them were from short-faced bears.

The Rancho La Brea Tar Pits are in Los Angeles, California. These pits are about 40,000 years old. They are full of sticky stuff called asphalt. Over the years, animals got stuck in the asphalt and died. Their bones stayed there and became today's fossils.

The Page Museum in California displays
fossils found in the Rancho La Brea Tar Pits.

Fossils are very important. Scientists study fossils to learn about prehistoric animals. This is how people discover exciting animals like the short-faced bear.

This woolly mammoth fossil is helpful for scientists studying prehistoric animals.

Important Words

fossil remains of very old animals and plants commonly found in the ground. A fossil can be a bone, a footprint, or any trace of life.

Ice Age a period in Earth's history when ice covered parts of the world. The last Ice Age ended about 11,500 years ago.

predator an animal that hunts and eats other animals.

prehistoric describes anything that was around more than 5,500 years ago.

prey an animal that is food for another animal.

Web Sites

To learn more about short-faced bears, visit ABDO Publishing Company on the World Wide Web. Web sites about short-faced bears are featured on our Book Links page. These links are routinely monitored and updated to provide the most current information available.

www.abdopub.com

Index